E9135X

·R·A·C·I·S·M·

Yasmin Alibhai and Colin Brown

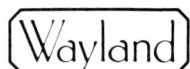

Points of View

Abortion
Advertising
Alcohol
Animal Rights
Censorship
Crime and Punishment
Divorce
Drugs

Medical Ethics
Northern Ireland
Nuclear Weapons
Pollution
Racism
Sex and Sexuality
Smoking
Terrorism

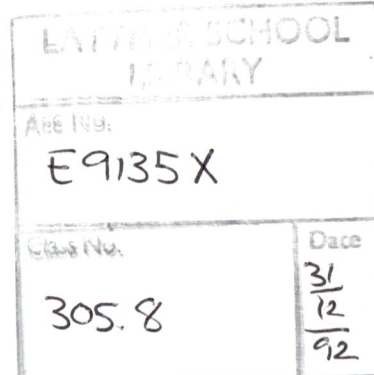

Front cover: A racist demonstration.

Editor: Paul Mason
Designer: David Armitage

First published in 1991 by
Wayland (Publishers) Limited
61 Western Road, Hove
East Sussex BN3 1JD, England

© Copyright 1991 Wayland (Publishers) Limited

British Library Cataloguing in Publication Data
Alibhai, Yasmin
 Racism. — (Points of view)
 I. Title II. Series
 305.8

ISBN 1 85210 651 4

Phototypeset by Direct Image Photosetting Ltd,
Hove, East Sussex, England.
Printed in Italy by G. Canale & C.SpA., Turin
Bound in France by A.G.M.

Acknowledgements

The publishers gratefully acknowledge permission from the following to reproduce copyright material: Allen Lane for an extract from *Man and the Natural World* by Keith Thomas; *Caribbean Times* for an extract from an article on race and class; the Commission for Racial Equality for extracts from *Five Views of Multi-Racial Britain* by Bhikhu Parekh and from the *Annual Report 1989*; *Daily Mail* for an extract from an article on equal opportunities policies; *Daily Telegraph* for an extract from 'A Ladder Out of the Ghetto' by Leon Hawthorne; Elektra Records/Tracey Chapman for an extract from 'Across the Lines' by Tracey Chapman; *The European* for an extract from 'Whose Europe is it Anyway?' by Jean Marie le Pen; Gower/Colin Brown for an extract from *Black and White Britain* by Colin Brown; *The Guardian* for an extract from 'Don't get lippy, Missy' by Angella Johnson; Harper and Row for an extract from *An American Dilemma* by Gunnar Myrdal; *The Independent* for extracts from 'The Untouchables of London's Suburbs', a report on immigration from Hong Kong by Nicholas Comfort and an article on the same subject by William Rees-Mogg; Institute of Race Relations for an extract from 'How Racism Came to Britain'; *Law Society Gazette* for an extract from an article by Geoffry Bindman; *Manchester Evening News* for an extract from a report on the stabbing of Ahmed Ullah; Manchester University Press for an extract from Bhikhu Parekh's introduction to *Strategies for Improving Race Relations* by John Shaw; Macmillan for an extract from *Politics and the Military in Uganda* by Amii Omara-Otunnu; The Monday Club for an extract from *Immigration, Repatriation and the Commission for Racial Equality* by Harvey Proctor and John Pinninger; New England Free Press for an extract from *An Analysis of American Racism* by Frank Joyce; *New Internationalist* for extracts from 'Racism Then and Now' by Paul Gordon and Chris Brazier and 'How to be Discriminating' by Mary Warren; *New Society* for extracts from 'The New Empire Within Britain' by Salman Rushdie and an article by Jane Lane of the CRE; *New Statesman and Society* for extracts from 'Canadian Club' by Yasmin Alibhai and 'The New Racism' by A. Sivanandan; *Newsweek* for an extract from 'Uninvited Guests' by Scott Sullivan; Penguin for extracts from *The Fire Next Time* by James Baldwin, *A Portrait of English Racism* by Anne Dummett, *Under Siege* by Keith Thompson and *A Seventh Man* by John Berger and Jean Mohr; Pluto Press for an extract from *Resistance to Rebellion* by A. Sivanandan; *Police Review*; Routledge and Kegan Paul for extracts from *Race and Racism* by Ruth Benedict; Runnymede Trust for extracts from *Race and Immigration*; Secker and Warburg for extracts from *Collected Works of Carl Jung*, and *Them* by Jonathan Green; *The Sun* for an extract from an article by Richard Littlejohn; *The Toronto Star* for extracts from articles by Leslie Papp and Royston James; The Trades Union Congress for an extract from Bill Morris's Preface to *Black Workers and Trade Unions*; Trentham for extracts from *The Black and White Media Book* by John Twitchin; Virago for extracts from *Conversations with Maya Angelou* by Jeffrey M. Elliot; *The Voice* for extracts from an article on the situation of Australian Aborigines and an article by Glory Osaji-Umeaku.

Contents

1. What is racism? — 4
2. Prejudice, racism and discrimination — 10
3. The roots of racism — 17
4. The experience of racism — 25
5. Racial justice and harmony — 31
6. Striving for equality — 36
7. Conclusions — 43

Glossary — 46

Further reading — 47

Contact addresses — 47

Index — 48

What is racism?

> *1st skinhead:* Do I condone it? Yes. They've got no right to be here.
> *Cohen (BBC reporter):* That families should have bricks thrown through the window, airgun pellets, that kind of thing?
> *1st skinhead:* Well, only blacks like, and Jews, yeh. White European race, right, is the superior race and always will be.
> *Cohen:* Is it really fair that families should be intimidated, after all, they are people?
> *1st skinhead:* Yes of course it is. They're not people, they are parasites, they're just poncing off us.
> *2nd skinhead:* I've just come out of prison myself, if I may say so, I just come out after doing fifteen months.
> *Cohen:* For doing what?
> *2nd skinhead:* Smashing a Pakistani up. I just stabbed him.
> (*File on 4*, BBC Radio Four, 25 February 1981.)

Why should anyone act in this way towards another person?

Groups of people who are perceived by others as sharing inherited characteristics — such as skin colour or hair type — are commonly referred to as races. Treating someone who is from a different race as though they are inferior to you is called racism. Years ago, races were seen as fundamental biological divisions of humankind, but scientific evidence has since disproved this theory. Races have been mixing and changing throughout history.

Below *Demonstrations against racial violence have been seen in Britain since the 1950s, when there were attacks on black immigrants. Teddy boys led those attacks. Groups like the British National Party (BNP) have taken up that hatred of blacks today.*

Black ghetto housing in the Bronx, New York — a typical scene in most big cities in the USA. What has happened to the land of plenty?

> Racism is essentially a pretentious way of saying that 'I' belong to the Best People. For such a conviction it is the most gratifying formula that has ever been discovered, for neither my own unworthiness nor the accusations of others can ever dislodge me from my position — a position which was determined in the womb of my mother at conception. It avoids all embarrassing questions about my conduct in life and nullifies all embarrassing claims by 'inferior' groups about their own achievements and ethical standards. (Ruth Benedict, *Race and Racism*, 1942.)

Racism is not just a thing that some individuals feel. Whole countries are racist in their policies. One of the worst consequences of this can be seen in the history of the USA:

> From the time the first Native American 'Indian' died at the hands of a European settler (if not before) the United States has held white supremacy as a dominant theme in its institutional and cultural life. The 'New World' civilization ultimately destroyed nearly one half of the 'Indian' population (genocide by any criteria), defined in its basic political document the black person as three fifths of a man, and created a chattel slavery system more dehumanizing and destructive than any the world has ever known. (Frank Joyce, *An Analysis of American Racism*.)

In Britain, racial minorities live in older, overcrowded, less desirable housing.
Dwellings with less than one room per person:
White 3 per cent
Afro-Caribbean 16 per cent
Asian 35 per cent
Dwellings built before 1945:
White owner-occupiers 56 per cent
Afro-Caribbean owner-occupiers 84 per cent
Asian owner-occupiers 81 per cent

Racism is not a new phenomenon. It has existed at least since European nations began to build empires abroad. Now, as before, it can be seen across the world.

> In the colonial empires of the British, French, Belgians, Germans and Dutch, racism [was used] to justify the ruthless exploitation of millions of people throughout the world. This plunder of natural and human resources financed industrial growth in Europe — and the notion that black people needed a firm white hand to guide them even allowed the Europeans to feel good about the theft. Colonialism is now over — but it is no longer necessary to rule others in order to exploit them. It is partly our racism, our enduring sense of black people as somehow inferior and uncivilized, which allows the rich world to go on exploiting the poor. ('Racism Then and Now', Paul Gordon and Chris Brazier, *New Internationalist,* March 1985.)

Slaves were traded and treated like animals. Millions were forced into labour, tortured and even killed by their owners. Many would claim the USA was built by these slaves, yet most black Americans remain second class citizens to this day.

What is racism?

A nationwide survey that involved Canadian police officers found these attitudes:
— More than one in five officers agreed 'some breeds of people are naturally better than others'.
— Some 73 per cent of officers agreed immigrants often bring discrimination on themselves.
— Fifty-six per cent said laws guaranteeing equal job opportunities already go too far. *(Toronto Star,* 15 January 1989.)

The origins of these colonial and post-colonial attitudes lie in the legacy of slavery, which reached its peak in the eighteenth century.

> The whites running the slave trade had to develop an argument which would allow them to be Christians and slave traders at the same time. Difficult? They managed it . . . 'A slave is a thing, a commodity, a piece of property — to be owned, used, disposed of. It has no history except at its point of entry into the market, no definition except on a bill of sale.'
> . . . And since they were commodities — things to be bought and sold and thrown away when done with — and not humans, they had no place beside the white men, on earth or in 'heaven'. (Institute of Race Relations, *How Racism Came to Britain,* 1985.)

Within a country, hostility of the majority towards a minority group is very often the basic component of racism, as in the treatment of blacks in America, but not always. A minority group with sufficient power can use racism to preserve its position — like white people in South Africa.

But isn't racism these days the responsibility of a few extremists?

> Most Americans get awfully uptight about the charge of racism, since most people are not conscious of what racism is. Racism is not a desire to get up every morning and lynch a black man from a tall tree. It is not engaging in vulgar epithets. These kinds of people are just fools. It is the day to day indignities, the subtle humiliations, that are so devastating. (Whitney Young, *Exceptional Children,* 1970.)

Some people, however, say that the effects of racism are overestimated. They claim that the so-called victims of racism are actually responsible for their situation:

> Our ethnic minorities are not 'victims of the system' . . . Prejudice undoubtedly exists — although it is by no means confined to the majority population. But the determining factor in a group's fortunes is not prejudice but the group's own cultural values. (Ray Honeyford, letter to *The Independent,* 18 October 1990.)

In Britain, racial minorities suffer worse unemployment.
Unemployment rate, 1984:
White men and women
    11 per cent
Men and women from racial minorities 21 per cent
Unemployment rate, 1989:
White men and women
    7 per cent
Men and women from racial minorities 12 per cent

So how do we know that racism exists? Evidence of racism and its effects emerges in many ways — in political speeches, newspaper articles, jokes and personal comments.

After the Second World War, many Arabs and Africans emigrated to France from the ex-French colonies because of acute economic problems in their own countries after decolonization. Europe needed cheap labour, to rebuild itself after the devastation of the war. After fifty years, the immigrant-descended population is still confined to the worst jobs and houses.

> Have you heard the one about the Indian doctor who moved in next door: he told me he was a better man than I was. I said why's that? He said at least he didn't have a Paki living next door to him.
>
> I had a friend who went to Africa to help the hungry – they ate him. (Bernard Manning, comedian, quoted in the *Daily Mail*, 2 May 1990.)

> Europe has become used to accepting unquestioningly millions of immigrants whose cultural, sanitary and professional level has done more harm than good. . . .
>
> Hundreds of millions of men and women are banging on our doors, and Europe cannot now 'receive all the misery of the world' . . . because it has failed – in Kipling's expression – to 'carry the white man's burden'. (Jean-Marie le Pen, Leader of the National Front in France, 'Whose Europe is it Anyway?', *The European*, 7 September 1990.)

When in work, racial minorities in Britain get worse jobs.
Percentage of employees with lower manual jobs:
White men 16
Afro-Caribbean men 36
Asian men 39
White women 32
Afro-Caribbean women 43
Asian women 46

What is racism?

Independent research, official government statistics and work by academics have shown repeatedly the extent and the damaging effects of racism.

> Australia's Aboriginals may soon become extinct if the racism against them is not dealt with, according to a new report. The World Council of Churches (WCC), holding its seventh world assembly in Canberra, produced a report on Australia's indigenous people... One of the towns that the WCC visited was Williannia in New South Wales where two-thirds of the 1,200 population are Aboriginal, most of whom are unemployed. Ironically, the only jobs many of Williannia's young Aboriginals have ever had were as extras in a feature film made in the town about the death of a young Aboriginal in police custody. (The Voice, 19 February 1991.)

> As we systematically compare the jobs, incomes, unemployment rates, private housing, local authority housing, local environments and other aspects of the lives of people with different ethnic origins, a single argument emerges... For the most part... Britain's well-established black population is still occupying the precarious and unattractive position of the earlier immigrants. (Colin Brown, *Black and White Britain*, 1984.)

---

1 Look at the dialogue at the beginning of the chapter – why do the skinheads feel they have the right to behave the way they do? What do you think of these reasons?

2 Is there a connection between history and present day racial attitudes?

3 List the kinds of racist behaviour you have seen, read about or experienced.

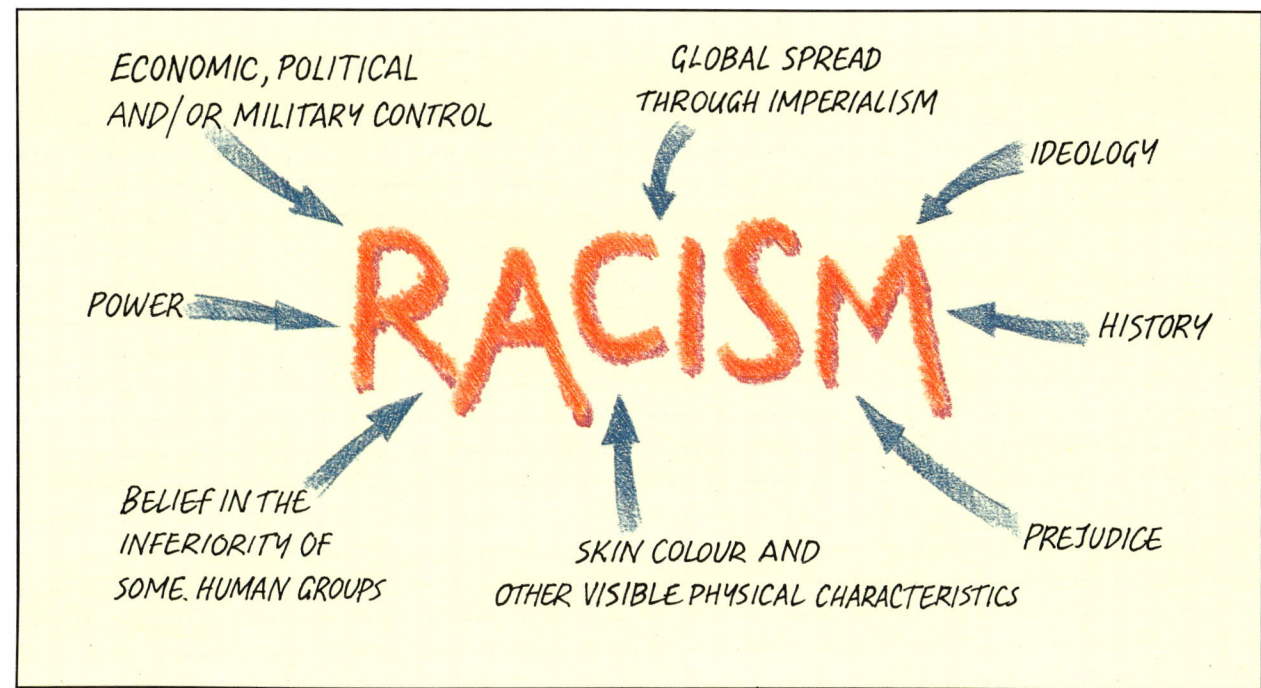

Prejudice, racism and discrimination

> Prejudice n. 1. an opinion formed beforehand, esp. an unfavourable one based on inadequate facts. 2. the act or condition of holding such opinions. 3. intolerance of or dislike for people of a specific race, religion, etc . . .
> (*The New Collins Concise Dictionary*, 1982.)

Why is there so much talk about racial prejudice when there are so many different sorts of prejudice?

> A white man may be prejudiced against a black man because he thinks he is lazy, sexy, dirty, mean, unclean, unintelligent, and so on, even as a black man might be prejudiced against a white man because in his view he is selfish, inhuman, merciless, devious, emotionally undeveloped, and the like. Since prejudice is based on some assumed characteristics of the victim, it can be countered by showing that he does not in fact possess that characteristic . . . Racism belongs to a very different category. It involves a total refusal to accept the victim as a full human being . . . and implies that his belonging to a particular race has so corrupted his humanity that he belongs to an entirely different species. (Bhikhu Parekh, Professor of Political Theory, 'Asians in Britain: Problem or Opportunity', *Five Views of Multi-Racial Britain*, Commission for Racial Equality, 1978.)

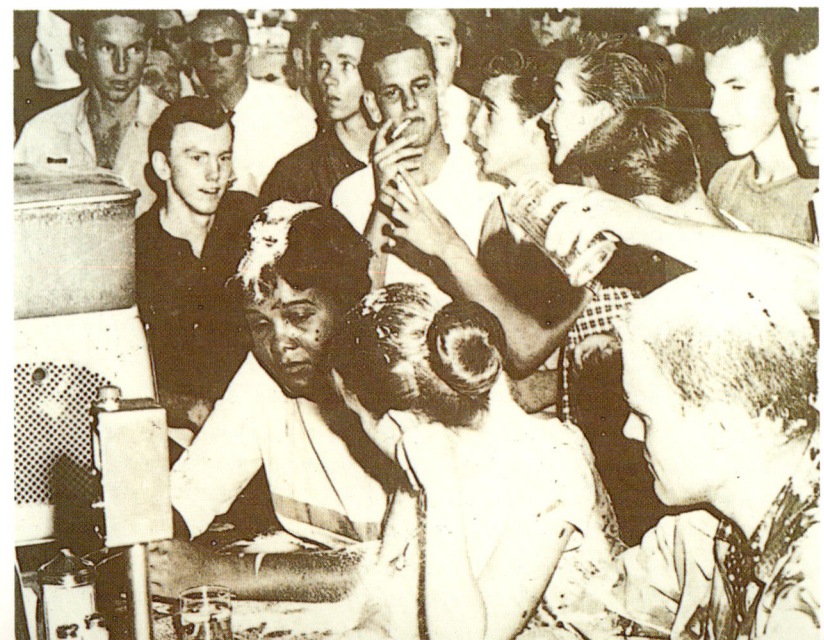

These Civil Rights campaigners in the USA during the 1960s are being humiliated in an all-white bar by white racists.

These are British High Court judges; some of the people who hold power in Britain. What does that mean for black Britons? Is it important to have more blacks in powerful positions?

Although we talk about racism as a general term, to be accurate we should say that it differs from racial prejudice. Racial prejudice is one person disliking another because he or she is black: to understand racism you have to look at the general situation of black people. If you look at the information boxes in the opening chapter, you will see that black people generally have worse housing, less chance of getting a job, and worse jobs if they do get one.

> ... the Negro's experience of the white world cannot possibly create in him any respect for the standards by which the white world claims to live ... white people, who had robbed black people of their liberty and who profited by this theft every hour that they lived, had no moral ground on which to stand. [But they] had the judges, the juries, the shotguns, the law – in a word, power ... those virtues preached but not practised by the white world were merely another means of holding Negroes in subjection [powerless]. (James Baldwin, *The Fire Next Time*, 1964.)

Thousands of Asians who had made their lives in Uganda were forced to leave the country, without any of their possessions and with no idea where they were going to end up. In the countries they went to, many politicians and members of the public resented their arrival and they were caught between two countries, neither of which wanted them. In a state of shock and despair when they arrived, many of them had to live in refugee camps for months before gradually making new lives for themselves.

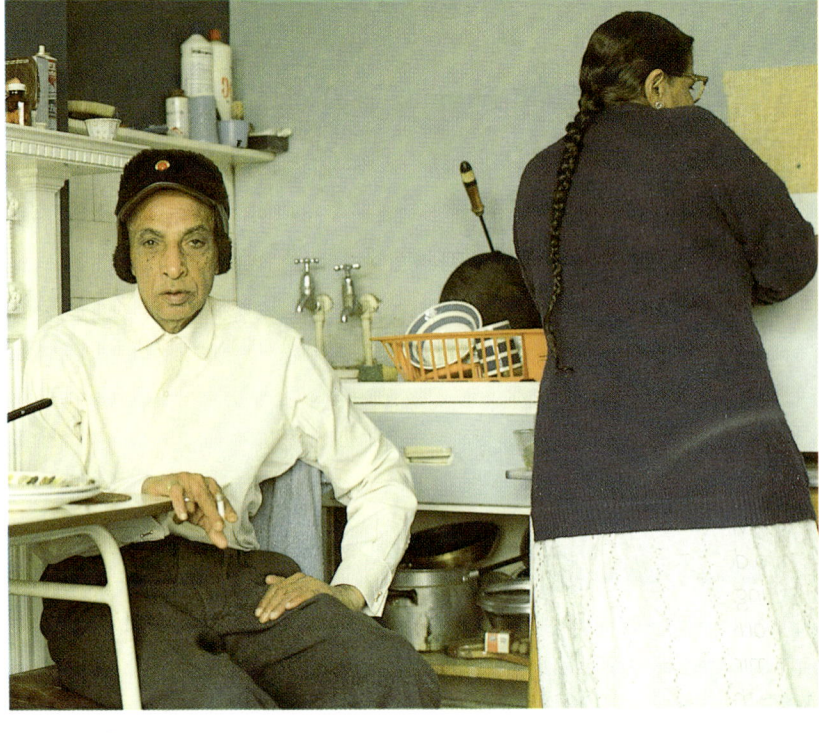

What about black racism? Is there such a thing? Although terrible prejudices can be seen all round the world between non-white people, those prejudices rarely combine with an ideology of racial inferiority and the power to spread it — two important characteristics of racism. And black people's prejudice is not rooted in a history of owning slaves and being taught to see blacks as inferior. People have often given ex-Ugandan President Idi Amin as an example of black racism, because he expelled Asians from Uganda.

> The regime [in Uganda] had gauged the attitude of the indigenous population aright: the Asians were unpopular because they derived their wealth not from agriculture but from trade, and as such they were perceived as economically exploitative as well as culturally exclusive ... On 4 August Amin announced that all Asians holding British passports and nationals of India, Pakistan and Bangla Desh were to go back to their countries ... (Amii Omara-Otunnu, *Politics and the Military in Uganda 1890-1985*, 1987.)

Amin's actions were based on jealousy, rather than on a notion that Asians were inferior to Africans, so it is inaccurate to call them racist.

In a special test, job applications were made to 300 employers in three English cities in 1985. In each case, there was one white applicant, one Asian applicant and one Afro-Caribbean applicant. Their qualifications and experience were the same. The results showed that a third of the employers discriminated against non-white applicants. The same test ten years earlier had produced exactly the same result.

Prejudice, racism and discrimination

Some people point out that the Hindu caste system in India is, like racism, based on a hierarchy of human beings determined at birth.

> The Hindu religion contains four main castes: the priests (Brahmins), warriors, artisans/merchants and labourers. Within the Sudra, or labourers' caste, there are as many as 3,700 subcastes. This complex hierarchy is believed to have developed from the time when fair-skinned Aryan conquerors subjugated the dark indigenous tribes of southern India. Untouchables ... are deemed so low that they are placed outside the caste system, along with animals and insects. ('The Untouchables of London's Suburbs', *The Independent*, 10 January 1991.)

> There is a lot of talk about race in Britain, but in India caste is race, people here don't understand that. I have been here 27 years, but even talking about this matter is almost physically painful to me. When someone calls me untouchable I feel as though it is a crime against me. (Prem Kumar Jhal, *The Times*, 6 July 1990.)

Below *In India, the caste system has meant wretched lives for millions of people who are considered to be the lowest of the low. Known as untouchables, these people are often to be found living in the streets, able only to do dirty jobs like lavatory cleaning. They are often victims of vicious attacks and discrimination by those who are above the untouchables in the caste hierarchy.*

Above *The advantages of belonging to the ruling classes in the colonies. A British colonialist and his wife in an animal skin boat serviced by 'coolies'.*

    Although the caste system defends a religious belief in inherited inferiority, it has not had the power to spread through the world as an ideology like white racism. It has had no empire to carry caste as an excuse for exploitation, as racism has. People argue that the violence and hatred now produced by the caste system are actually colonial imports from the West.

> The caste system has become the scapegoat for the contemporary evil of class hatred imported into India or among Indians elsewhere, from the West. There is no record of any caste conflict in India before the present age ... What is really pernicious is that class hatred is permeating the old caste distinctions, in which there was no room for hatred. Hatred among men is not a Hindu passion, but one that is European. (Nirad Chaudhury, letter to the *Daily Telegraph*, 15 October 1990.)

Prejudice, racism and discrimination

Treating someone unfairly because of their race is called racial discrimination. This can be blatant, or it can be hidden.

> Racism is so polite in this country. They don't say 'No Niggers'. They smile and tell you the house or the job has just gone — sometimes minutes after you phone. (Wilson Head, black President of the Urban League in Canada, quoted in 'Canadian Club', Yasmin Alibhai, *New Statesman and Society*, 2 September 1988.)

Racism works differently in different countries. In South Africa, for example, where blacks are not allowed to elect members of the law-making bodies, racism is enshrined in the constitution. In the USA, the legacy of slavery produced an insidious and vicious kind of racism:

> When white terrorists bomb a black church and kill five black children, that is an act of individual racism, widely deplored by most sections of society. But when in that same city — Birmingham, Alabama — 500 black babies die because of a lack of proper food, shelter and medical facilities, and thousands more are destroyed and marred physically, mentally and intellectually because of conditions of poverty and discrimination in the black community, that is a function of institutional racism. (Stokely Carmichael and Charles V. Hamilton, *Black Power: The Politics of Liberation in America*, 1969.)

The South Bronx in New York. Many black and Hispanic children in the USA are born into this hard, deprived environment, with appalling housing, poor education, bad health care and no prospects. The situation has not improved for decades. Is it any wonder that violence, the drug culture and other problems take root in these areas?

This homeless black child sleeping on a fruit box in front of an air vent was photographed in one of the richest countries in the world – South Africa.

In Britain racism stems from the attitudes of cultural and political superiority which sustained the empire:

> If you want to understand British racism – and without understanding, no improvement is possible – it is impossible even to begin to grasp the nature of the beast unless you accept its historical roots; unless you see that 400 years of conquest and looting, centuries of being told that you are superior to the fuzzy-wuzzies and the wogs, leave their stain on you all; that such a stain seeps into every part of your culture, your language and your daily life ... (Salman Rushdie, 'The New Empire Within Britain', *New Society*, 9 December 1982.)

Although the variations between countries are important, there is much in common between the experiences of black people in different parts of the world when they encounter white people:

> I thought the British were a nice people, a friendly people, until I began looking for a job and looking for a room. Then I began meeting the racism. And that began to bring into myself something new: I began to start understanding my roots on a global level. I had left the parochialism of South African politics and what I had experienced there now had a global setting. (Bennie Bunsie, an Indian who migrated from South Africa to England, quoted in Jonathan Green, *Them*, 1990.)

1 Is there a difference between racism and (a) caste conflicts; (b) conflicts between groups of black African people?

3

The roots of racism

From the end of the seventeenth century onwards, various theologians, writers and scientists defined black people as inferior, bestial and less than human.

> Robert Gray declared in 1609, that 'the greater part' of the earth was 'possessed and wrongfully usurped by wild beasts ... or by brutish savages, which by reason of their godless ignorance, and blasphemous idolatry, are worse than those beasts' ... 'Their words are sounded rather like that of apes than men', reported Sir Thomas Herbert of the inhabitants of the Cape of Good Hope; 'I doubt that many of them have no better predecessors than monkeys' ... 'The Hottentots,' thought a Jacobean clergyman, were, 'beasts in the skin of man' and their speech 'an articulate noise rather than language, like the clucking of hens or gabbling of turkeys.' They were 'filthy animals,' said a later traveller, who 'hardly deserved the name of rational creatures.' (Keith Thomas, *Man and the Natural World*, 1983.)

This picture of a San ('bushman') in South Africa was taken in 1904. There has always been an interest in the West in 'strange and barbaric' people around the world – an interest still popular amongst journalists and academics. The problem is they rarely see these people as equals.

The psychoanalyst Carl Jung, writing in the early twentieth century, also believed white people to be innately more advanced than black people.

> There is a much better hypothesis to explain the peculiarities of the American temperament. It is the fact that the States are pervaded by the Negro, that most striking and suggestive figure... What is more contagious than to live side by side with a rather primitive people? Go to Africa and see what happened... the inferior man has a tremendous pull over our psyche which has lived through untold ages of similar conditions... (Carl Jung, *Collected Works, Vol X*, 1927.)

It was and is possible to maintain these beliefs only by taking a very one-sided view of history, of science, and of culture. If one takes an equally one-sided view from the opposite perspective, it is just as easy to 'prove' that non-white peoples have over the centuries had the most progressive role in human development.

> From ancient Egypt, from the oldest world civilization, came the scientific and technological knowledge, the religious ideas and cultural, artistic contributions which shaped the earliest cultures of the European world. The day when the Africans and blacks will impose that point of view, a view supported by scientifically verifiable historical data, the self image of blacks and the warped image others have construed of blacks will have to undergo a most profound revision. (Chiekh Anta Diop, interviewed in *Africascope*, February 1977.)

America was not discovered by Europeans. There was already a population of Native Americans, who welcomed their white guests at first. But the ambitions of the Europeans required more than peaceful settlement, and within a few years of their arrival the immigrants had virtually destroyed the original population of North America and confined the rest to reservations. They remain there, poor and degraded.

> Perhaps we describe this civilization of ours as built on steel and gunpowder. But steel was invented either in India or in Turkestan, and gunpowder in China. Perhaps we prefer to identify our Western culture by its printing presses and literateness. But paper and printing were both borrowed from China. (Ruth Benedict, *Race and Racism*, 1942.)

The oldest civilizations in the world occurred in the Middle East and Africa. Why then have these places come to be regarded by some in the West as backwards and barbaric?

• Scapegoats

When there are problems in a society, like a shortage of housing and high unemployment, people tend to want someone to blame. It is easy to point to someone who looks different and say everything is their fault.

> If you dislike or resent a particular group to begin with, you will pick up on some characteristics about them to dislike ... There may be two identical middle-income houses in one street, in one of which an English family live, with their married daughter, husband and children in rather cramped conditions, while in the other, a Jamaican family live in identical circumstances. The usual way to refer to the two households is that the Jamaican house is overcrowded ('once they're in they bring all their relations in and turn it into a slum') while at the other house the Robinsons have had to take in their daughter's family because they can't get a house. (Anne Dummett, *A Portrait of English Racism*, 1973.)

It is not just the physical differences but also the cultures of black people that are resented and despised. This resentment and hatred is not just confined to a few thugs and extreme right wing groups. It is found among journalists, newspaper and magazine editors, media personalities and many prominent politicians as well. This statement was made by Margaret Thatcher only months before she became prime minister of Britain.

> ...I think...that people are really rather afraid that this country might be swamped by people with a different culture.

The roots of racism

Above *The ex-British prime minister, Margaret Thatcher, who was ready to excuse racism as concern for the 'British character' being 'swamped'.*

And you know, the British character has done so much for democracy, for law, and so much throughout the world, that if there is a fear that it might be swamped, people are going to react, and be rather hostile to those coming in. (Margaret Thatcher, MP, speaking in 1978.)

● The media

The media play a central part in determining how black people are perceived:

> Of all the pictures I have seen of 'Band Aid' and its 'subsidiaries' the one that sticks out in my mind is the one of Bob Geldof, KBE, looking like a latter day Lawrence of Arabia, walking in the desert with hundreds of black hands tugging at his robes — welcoming this white saviour in their midst... They are portrayed as passive and helpless, spectators to their own destiny — the West is the superior partner... it can reinforce in some British people's minds the idea that black immigrants here are fleeing economic hardship from their own poverty stricken countries. They are the 'needy outsiders who take up jobs, scrounge off social security and live in luxury off the council etc.' (Zeinab Badawi, TV newsreader, 'Reflections on Recent TV Coverage of Africa', in John Twitchin (ed.), *The Black and White Media Book*, 1988.)

Newspapers also resort to racist images of people, particularly at times of national conflict. During the period leading up to the war with Iraq, a popular British newspaper printed this in one of its opinion columns:

> What I can live without are British women married to Iraqis, arriving back at Heathrow and Gatwick... in full Arab garb and complaining about Mrs Thatcher's 'aggression' in the Middle East. They have chosen to turn their back on Britain, our values and beliefs. They should be left to rot in their adopted country with their hideous husbands and their unattractive children. (Richard Littlejohn, *The Sun*, 18 September 1990.)

● Immigration

One controversial area on which the media has concentrated is the issue of immigration. Immigration controls of people from the world's poor countries are the subject of heated debate.

Left *The celebrity Bob Geldof (in black), who helped to raise millions of pounds for relief work in Ethiopia and the Sudan. The causes of famine and poverty in the world's poor countries are complex. Black people in these countries are often the victims of global politics, history, corrupt politicians and economic exploitation. But the images of black victims being saved by generous and efficient whites continue the myth that black people are not capable of looking after themselves.*

> A couple of years ago, the British press made a huge stink about a family of African Asians who arrived at Heathrow airport and were housed by a very reluctant local authority. It became a classic media witchhunt: 'They come over here, sponge off the state and jump the housing queue'. But that same week, another family also landed at Heathrow, also needing, and getting, housing from the local authority. The second family barely made the papers... It was a family of white Rhodesians running away from the prospect of a free Zimbabwe. (Salman Rushdie, 'The New Empire Within Britain', *New Society*, 9 December 1982.)

European immigration laws often reinforce racism by permitting the entry of white people, even if they are from the same country as black people who are being excluded.

Above and **right** *The British government invited black people to Britain in the 1950s and 1960s because their labour was needed for the expanding transport and health services. The men on the right are on the first immigrant ship, the Windrush. Without the immigrants the post-war recovery of Britain would have been much slower. They came with great expectations. Most ended up deeply disappointed.*

Right *Hong Kong. It is well known that immigrants are often enterprising and hard working people who contribute enormously to the economy. Canada and the USA have benefited greatly from having large numbers of European immigrants who went there after the Second World War. Could the Hong Kong Chinese help inject new energy into the British economy if given a chance to move to Britain?*

> Tension between European natives and their 'guest workers' has existed since the early 1970s. But the last 5 years have brought a sharp acceleration of racism and xenophobia across the face of Western Europe. Immigrants are regularly blamed for every conceivable social ill, from straining the resources of the welfare state to drug dealing and terrorism ... And the issue now threatens to derail the European Community's ambitious project to eliminate frontiers between its member states by the end of 1992. To a large extent, the explosive issue feeds on perceptions rather than fact. Legal immigration from non-European countries into West Germany, Britain and France has slowed to a trickle since 1975. (Scott Sullivan, 'Uninvited Guests', *Newsweek*, 5 February 1990.)

Surveys repeatedly show that the majority of the British population remains hostile to non-white immigration. When changes in the future government of Hong Kong made it likely that some of its citizens would come to Britain, there was immediate opposition to their entry:

> Two in every three voters oppose the Government's Bill to give 50,000 Hong Kong Chinese families the right to settle in Britain according to a poll conducted this weekend for *The Independent on Sunday* ... The poll also shows overwhelming public support, 84 per cent, for further curbs on immigration, over and above present restrictions. (Nicholas Comfort, *Independent on Sunday*, 8 April 1990.)

Politicians like Jean Marie le Pen have used racism to gain popularity and power.

Others express the view that such narrow-mindedness is against the national interest, stressing the economic issues.

> There is no more hard-working, peaceable or useful community in Britain [than the Chinese community]. There is no case for supposing that another 50,000 Chinese families, if they came, would be other than 50,000 additions to the general well-being of our society and to our economic capacity in a competitive world. (William Rees-Mogg, *The Independent*, 9 April 1990.)

Politicians add more fuel to the racists' fire:

> Two million unemployed. That's two million immigrants too many... We establish a direct link with the presence in France of more than 6 million immigrants who live at the expense of the French working population. (Jean-Marie le Pen, leader of the National Front in France, election speech, 1986.)

> We must be mad, literally mad as a nation, to be permitting the annual inflow of some 50,000 dependants who are for the most part the material of the future growth of the immigrant descended population. It is like watching a nation busily engaged in heaping up its own funeral pyre. (Enoch Powell, MP, speech in Birmingham, 1968.)

---

1 Do you disagree that the character of a nation can be 'swamped' by immigrants? Why?

2 Reread the statement by Richard Littlejohn, from **The Sun**, on page 21. There are laws in Britain against incitement to racial hatred: why do you think he was not prosecuted?

3 What are the issues in this chapter that most moved, surprised or angered you? Why?

4

The experience of racism

> I began to come into contact with racism at school. You'd hear some snidey remarks. There was this rhyme: 'Pal meat for dogs, Kit-e-Kat for wogs'. Stupid little things, but terrible. (Michael de Souza, black youth worker, quoted in Jonathan Green, *Them*, 1990.)

It is often said that the jokey use of racist insults is offensive. But are people being oversensitive, and carrying a chip on their shoulder?

> I simply adore this place. Prejudice is simply part of human nature, but really the English are very tolerant. I would never have received elsewhere the sort of welcome as day to day in my life I receive in this country. (Om Parmar, Asian businessman in Birmingham, Britain, quoted in the *Birmingham Post*, 9 May 1990.)

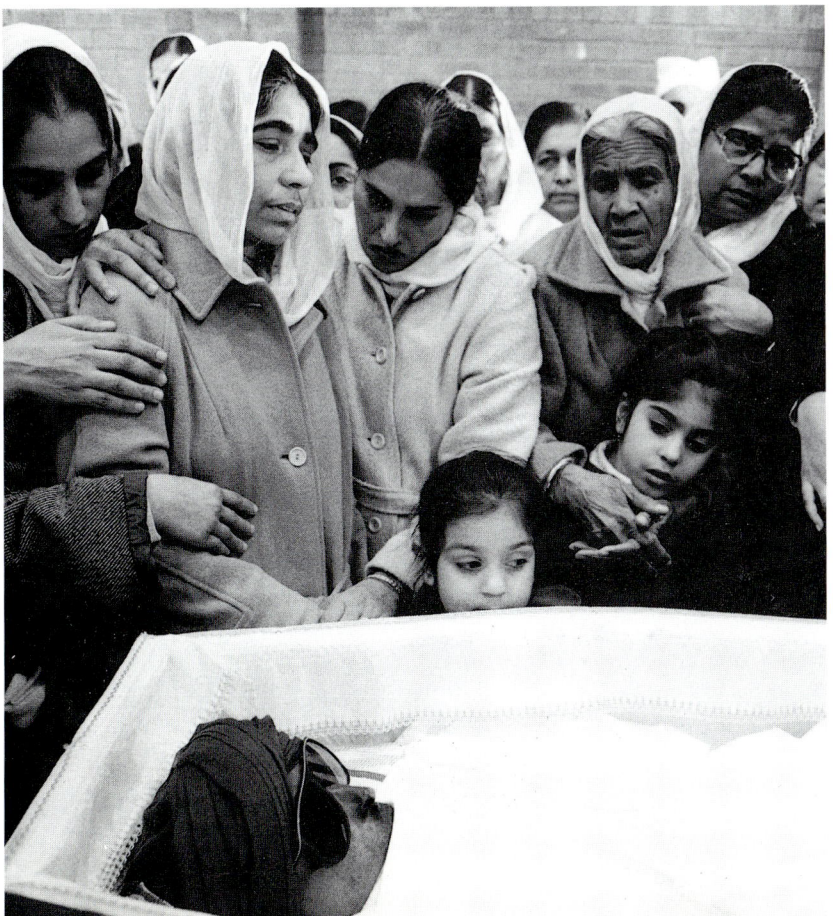

Above and **left** *Although notices such as the one above saying, 'No coloured men,' are now illegal, other sorts of racism continue. Emotions ran high at the funeral in 1990 of Kuldip Singh Sekhon, shown on the left. He was an Asian taxi driver in Southall, West London. Sekhon had fifty stab wounds — the work, many believe, of a racist gang. This tragic picture of his wife and children shows the consequences of such senseless violence.*

25

But are racist jokes really so harmless?

> Racist jokes may seem to some people a trivial matter. But they belong to a spectrum of racially inflammatory speech which in different degrees may be both dangerous and damaging. It seems inevitable that racist jokes told publicly by adults encourage young people to accept that racial hostility is acceptable, even admirable ... racial incitement is bound to lead to racial violence — that must indeed be its purpose. (Geoffrey Bindman, *The Law Society Gazette No. 36*, 10 October 1990.)

The effect of legitimizing racism through television has been studied by academics. Research in 1967 found that children aged over ten get their attitudes more from reading and watching television than from their parents:

> A case in point is the influence of the TV series 'Love Thy Neighbour' which portrayed a white bigot who heaps racial abuse upon his neighbour. The programme was meant to be funny ... A primary school headteacher in Fyfe, Scotland said that children in his school 'had made a coloured worker's life a misery, calling him names like 'coon' and 'sambo', having picked them up from the programme ...'. (Gajendra Verma, 'Attitudes, Race Relations and Television', in John Twitchin, *The Black and White Media Book*, 1988.)

Spike Lee, a young black film maker who rose to prominence in the 1980s with highly acclaimed films like Do the Right Thing. *He is one of a new generation of talented blacks successfully challenging prejudiced and stereotyped views of black people. He runs a workshop for young black Americans and is not afraid to take up controversial themes in his films. Lee is often contrasted to figures like Eddie Murphy, who many feel has become a token black actor used by Hollywood to perpetuate old images.*

The experience of racism

Racism in personal relations is hurtful and demeaning, but the experience of discrimination when looking for employment has even more serious consequences. People are denied the right to earn their living. This means that they are denied the right to good housing, clothing and food, because they cannot afford them.

> When I turned up to start work the personnel officer said 'I'm terribly sorry, you're such a nice person, but I'm afraid we can't have you working here at all'. So I asked, 'Why not?' He said: 'The other girls have got up a petition: we can only take you on if we provide a separate lavatory for you'. (Simi Bedford, black TV journalist, quoted in Jonathan Green, *Them*, 1990.)

> A study of 672 corporate and employment agency employees across Canada released last spring showed deep discrimination against visible minorities. More than 80 per cent of the corporate headhunters and all job agency recruiters surveyed said they received direct requests that discriminated by race. Ninety-four per cent said they had discriminated against job seekers on the basis of colour... In a 1985 federally funded study it was found that white job applicants were three times more likely to be hired than blacks with the same credentials. (Leslie Papp and Royson James, in the *Toronto Star*, 16 January 1989.)

In South Africa the actual experience of racism for black people continues to blight their lives. Angella Johnson, a black European journalist, recently tried to get on a bus in the capital, Pretoria.

> The white bus driver's eyes widened in astonishment as I boarded... 'You can't ride on here', he blustered. I asked why not. 'We don't carry your kind. You must get off', he replied... He looked contemptuously at my fare on the till counter. 'This bus is for white people only. I can't carry you.' I held my ground. 'Do I have to **put** you off?' he said through clenched teeth, climbing out of his booth in a threatening manner. My heart started pounding. It was the first of many occasions during my visit to South Africa that I was to experience blatant and aggressive racial prejudice for attempting to cross the barriers which still divide this colour-coded country. (Angella Johnson, 'Don't get lippy, missy', *The Guardian*, 9 May 1990.)

A world injustice
- In the USA, black American children are twice as likely to die before the age of 12 months as children born into white families.
- In Canada, suicides among Native Americans in the 15-24 years age group are 6 times the national average, and they are 7 times more likely to be imprisoned than the general population.
- In the UK, black people are 50-60 times more likely than whites to be victims of racial attacks.
- In New Zealand, Maoris are four times as likely as non-Maoris to be unemployed.
- In Australia, only 3 per cent of the Aboriginal population lives in housing on par with normal white Australian standards and 80 per cent have no educational qualifications. ('Outside the Circle: The denial of minority rights', *New Internationalist No. 128*, October 1983.)

Violent attacks motivated by racial hatred have also been a constant danger for racial minorities throughout the world, and there is evidence that they are increasing. At its worst, racism claims lives. People of all ages have died in fires and assaults because of the colour of their skins.

> On the night of 25 January 1982 a gang of forty attacked the home of the Saddique family in the East End of London. They threw stones, smashing the shop windows and narrowly missing the family crouched inside in darkness. They daubed swastikas, gave Nazi salutes and chanted ... They did this for six straight hours without intervention from the police. Nasreen, the eldest daughter, then aged 14, wrote in her diary: 'When the trouble started, we phoned the police, but they never came ...'. The entries in Nasreen's diary for the days, weeks, months and years that followed, often written by candlelight or in freezing darkness as the family huddled in an upstairs room, were repetitive and to the point. (John Pilger, foreword to Keith Thompson, *Under Siege: Racism and Violence in Britain Today,* 1988.)

Black people are often made into scapegoats by extreme right wing groups and blamed for job shortages and other problems. These problems are then used to fuel white hostility to blacks.

This is a British family. Why should they be terrorized by racial abuse and attacks? Asians are fifty times and Afro-Caribbeans thirty-six times more likely to be assaulted than white people, according to official statistics. What is the likely long-term effect on black people when they have to live in fear and with this kind of hatred? Are white people who feel this hatred also damaged by it?

> On 17th September 1986, 13-year-old Ahmed Ullah went to the aid of an Asian boy who was being taunted and bullied by white youths in the grounds of Burnage High School, Manchester. Ahmed was stabbed to death with a knife by a 13-year-old boy who had earlier boasted: 'I am going to have a "Paki fight", I am going to kill him.' *(Manchester Evening News, 7 February 1987.)*

Victims of racial attacks often complain that the police do not do enough to help them or to catch their assailants. The police say they take the problem seriously but that many victims fail to report these crimes, or even lie about them.

> For heaven's sake, we don't want women and kids burned to death while we do nothing about it, but there are a lot of factors within the Asian community that make it convenient for them to allege racial motivation when it's simply caste or money at the root of the problem. We could find a real racist much more quickly if we were told the truth every time. (Editorial, *Police Review*, November 1989.)

A free and pleasant land?
In Britain, black people are more likely to go to prison than whites in spite of having fewer previous convictions. They are more likely to be taken to court, rather than cautioned, even for first offences.
14 per cent of British prisoners are black or Asian, compared with less than 5 per cent of the general population. (From *Black People and the Criminal Justice System*, National Association for the Care and Resettlement of Offenders, May 1988.)

These youths in East London are demonstrating against police inaction on racial violence.

Racism can also affect the way the police and the courts deal with people. Much of police work depends on their personal handling of situations and on their quick assessment of people, so there is a high risk of racial prejudice and stereotypes influencing their actions.

> Norman Brown of North York [Ontario, Canada] saved for several years to import a sports car from the United States. On his first weekend of driving the sleek, eye-catching machine he was stopped four times by the police. He was not given a ticket. Officers 'were just inquisitive,' he says. 'They wanted to know what a black man's doing driving a car like this. Every time I drive by, they look at me hard'. (Leslie Papp and Royson James, in the *Toronto Star*, 14 January 1989.)

The experience of racism has devastated some cultures. This is what a Maori woman wrote recently about the plight of her people:

> Even though in a different time scale, our treatment by European invaders also parallels that of Asia, Africa, and the Americas. We too have been subjected to genocide. We too have been victims of land alienation. We too have been decimated by the diseases of Europe. We too have been forced to carry our cultures within us and wear the culture of the European like a second skin. And today, we are second class citizens in our own homelands... (quoted in *Links 23*, 1986.)

---

1 Can you think of a television programme that was either racist itself or discussed racism as a problem?

2 How do you think you would feel if you were in Nazreen's place? Have you heard of Anne Frank, the Jewish girl who kept a diary while hiding from the Nazis during the war-time occupation of Amsterdam? Do you think they would have felt similarly?

3 From the statement made in Police Review on racial harassment, do you think the police are making excuses, or do you think they are caught in the middle of an impossible situation? Why should the 'root of the problem' affect the way they respond to the crime?

5

Racial justice and harmony

Why should we worry about racism, prejudice and discrimination? Aren't they just facts of life, all parts of human nature, and things we should just learn to live with?

● **Moral arguments**
> There can be no doubt that indulgence in racism and discrimination, whether produced by the morally bankrupt Botha regime in South Africa or by some back-street textile employer in Bradford, represents the greatest social evil of our time. The practice of discrimination on grounds of race actually debases humanity because it devalues its victims and corrupts its perpetrators. (Bill Morris, black British trade union leader, Preface to *Black Workers and Trade Unions*, 1986.)

In the USA, the rights of citizens spelt out in the Constitution are a source of national pride. But the treatment of black Americans has never matched those ideals. In 1944 the famous writer Gunnar Myrdal described the great moral dilemma in America as the inner conflict between the:
> ... ideals of equality, freedom, God given dignity of the individual, inalienable rights on the one hand, against practices of discrimination, humiliation, insult and denial of opportunity to Negroes and others in a racist society on the other. (Gunnar Myrdal, *An American Dilemma*, 1944.)

● **Economic arguments**
The wealth of North America has been generated by the hard work of the immigrants of many races who feed its labour pool. This is true in Europe too. Despite this, immigrants are too often seen as a burden rather than an asset.
> All the industrial countries of Europe employ and depend upon migrant labour... In France, 20% of all industrial workers are migrants, in Germany, 12%, in Switzerland, 40%. They are concentrated in the most disagreeable and less well paid jobs ... Migrants are widely termed *Zigeuner* (gypsy), *Lumpenpack* (rag pack), *Kameltreiber* (camel herder) or *Schlangenfresser* (snake eater). (Berger and Mohr, *A Seventh Man*, 1975.)

In 1991, Bill Morris was elected general secretary of one of the largest and most powerful unions in Britain (the TGWU) – the first black person ever to hold such high office in the Trade Union movement. What do you think this will mean to British workers?

Immigrants to America at the turn of the century. White immigrants have often found it hard to settle into a new country, but they are not always treated in the way black people are. Do you think there is any link between racism and immigration, or are they really separate issues?

Claims by racist politicians that these jobs rightly belong to white people ignore the undesirable nature of jobs and working conditions experienced by immigrants.

> Little has been written about the life and conditions of these workers in Britain . . . and even less is known about the crucial role they play in modern capitalism. But in Germany, Gunter Walraff, a journalist, lived in the guise of an illegal Turkish worker, 'Ali'. He exposed the plight of the 'lowest of the low' . . . Ali makes for the factories and building sites where he unblocks lavatories ankle-deep in piss and covered in racist graffiti; removes sludge from pipes atop tall buildings in 17 degrees of frost; shovels and inhales coke dust hour after hour below ground level . . . (A. Sivanandan, 'The New Racism', *New Statesman and Society,* 4 November 1988.)

● Democratic rights

Democracy is based on the idea that every citizen of a country has an equal right to play a part in the political system, and is equal before the law. How can non-whites in democratic countries be systematically treated as second-class citizens?

> . . . a better America will be one which benefits not some groups alone but all citizens; so long as there is starvation and joblessness in the midst of abundance we are inviting the deluge. To avert it we must 'strongly resolve' that all men shall have the basic opportunity to work and to earn a living wage, that education and health and decent shelter shall be available to all, that regardless of race, creed, or colour, civil liberties shall be protected. (Ruth Benedict, *Race and Racism,* 1942.)

Racial justice and harmony

But is this a fair view? It can be argued that in a Western democracy, you make it to the top if you want to, and that those who don't are simply weak or inept. Success stories like Bill Cosby and Oprah Winfrey in the USA, and Asian millionaires in Britain, can be said to show what is possible.

Leon Hawthorne, a successful black journalist, said in an article in the *Daily Telegraph*, 20 June 1990, that his experience was proof that education is the key to success. He thinks that if blacks can succeed in it they will succeed anywhere. He also said that discrimination becomes less of a problem the further up the social ladder one gets, because it is hard for someone to treat you as inferior when you are more intelligent and richer than him. Hawthorne claimed that if you are black and ambitious and intelligent, there are no limits to how far you can get, but most young black people are resigned to the gutter of society. He said that they need a kick up the backside.

There are many non-whites who do succeed in this way. In the USA this success brings with it problems for the black community as a whole. Maya Angelou, a black American writer, is deeply worried:

> We are in a situation more dangerous than slavery. We are becoming polarised again, so there is a middle class, and a professional class and a working class, an underclass, a literate class, a drug class and an illiterate class. We have almost a steel floor between the middle and the underclasses, so strong that only a few can puncture it. (Maya Angelou, in Jeffrey M. Elliot, *Conversations with Maya Angelou*, 1989.)

Above *Famous blacks such as Oprah Winfrey, a chat show host, have succeeded against all odds and are important role models for many young blacks around the world.*

The placard means 'Rest in peace legal discrimination against foreigners.' For these Turkish immigrants to Germany it is still a dream: however long they stay and however much tax they pay, they are not entitled to any state benefits. Is this fair?

Leon Hawthorne's view is that racism is less serious among the middle classes. But studies show the opposite.

> Middle and upper income black people in the US say they encounter racism in their business and private lives more often than do black people in lower income strata, says a poll . . . Black people on higher incomes were more likely to perceive racism at work, while shopping or seeking housing, ir their dealings with the criminal justice system, in social settings in newspapers and on radio and TV. (*Caribbean Times*, 15 September 1989.)

> Black solicitors in England and Wales are treated by white colleagues as less competent than white solicitors, as a problem to employ because their colour might frighten off white clients and as an 'embarrassment' . . . Black solicitors also complained that they find it difficult to obtain articles, difficult to progress in firms once they have been taken on, and then difficult to be taken seriously by the legal establishment. (Report on *The Race Report* by the Law Society, in *Race and Immigration No. 226*, June 1989.)

Judge Clarence Thomas was nominated as a Supreme Court judge in 1991 by President Bush of the USA. Many liberals — black and white — thought he was a bad choice. This was because he held deeply conservative and hardline views on politics and crime. Does simply having someone black in a position of power help defeat racism?

Advertisements like this one by Benetton try to use images of racial harmony to promote their goods. Some people object to them because they do not give a true picture of the unequal relationship between black and white people. Others say that by showing blacks and whites together Benetton are presenting a positive image. What do you think?

● **Peace, or equal rights?**

Most people only become aware of race relations problems when racial discrimination leads to trouble in the streets or in the courts. But an absence of open racial conflict does not mean an absence of racial discrimination.

> For some the racial question is about how to create love and goodwill between blacks and whites and enable them to live in harmony. [But] love has no meaning outside the world of intimate interpersonal relationships, and is a politically irrelevant and unrealisable goal. As for racial harmony, it is a vague and indeterminate concept. Further, when relations between two groups are unequal and conflictual, the language of harmony only subserves the interests of the dominant group. (Bhikhu Parekh, Professor of Political Theory, Preface to John W. Shaw et al, *Strategies for Improving Race Relations*, 1987.)

> People's attitudes don't mean a damn to me, but it matters to me if I can't send my child to the school I want to send my child to, if I can't get the job for which I am qualified and so on . . . Racism is about power and not about prejudice. That is what we learnt in the years of struggle in the 1960s – when we met it in the trade unions, on the shop floor, in the community, at the ports of entry. We learnt it as we walked the streets, in the social and welfare services, in the health service – we learnt it everywhere. (A. Sivanandan, 'British Racism: The road to 1984', *Race and Class*, 1984.)

1 Discuss the major arguments about how we need to deal with racism put forward in this chapter. Which one makes most sense to you? Do you think people of a different race would feel differently?

2 What do you think makes successful blacks dismiss the effect of racism?

6 Striving for equality

Even if we accept that racial injustice is pervasive in many societies and that it does need to be tackled, how can we strive for equality in an unfair world?

● **Education**

Some see education as the key to reducing prejudice and discrimination in the future.

> We would not wish our [white] children to grow up to be racially prejudiced and discriminate against black people, and we would not wish our black children to be subjected to such prejudice and have their lives limited by racial discrimination. I wish to argue that unless we make positive plans and adopt strategies, then by default this is likely to happen. (Jane Lane of the Commission for Racial Equality, *New Society*, 4 December 1987.)

In racially mixed areas changes are taking place. This is a community group in London.

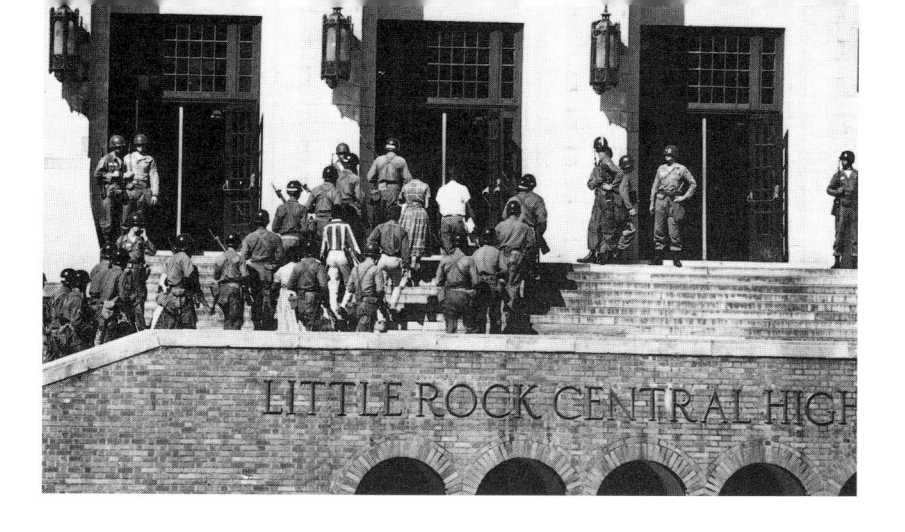

In the mid-1950s, segregated education in the USA officially ended. But when the first black pupils went to previously white schools the anger felt by whites was so overwhelming that troops had to be used to escort black students in and out of school. They could not stop the harrassment though, and it was years before mixed schools were accepted.

But some parents even oppose the mixing of races in schools. In the 1950s, when segregation of white and black schooling was first outlawed in the USA, a politician stated the case against mixing as follows:

> Separation promotes racial harmony. It permits each race to follow its own pursuits, to develop its own culture, its own institutions, its own civilization ... In fact, segregation is desired and supported by the vast majority of the members of both of the races of the South, who dwell side by side under harmonious conditions. (Senator James O. Eastland, speech in US Senate, 27 May 1954.)

More recently in Britain, there have been a number of highly publicized cases of white parents taking their children out of multi-racial schools.

> A group of parents who have been refusing since last September to send their children to Headfield School, where most of the children are of Asian origin, won the right to send the children to a school of their choice ... *(Race and Immigration No. 218, September 1988.)*

This kind of white reaction against ethnic minority cultures has been supported by some politicians and journalists who see diversity and anti-racist teaching as dangerous.

> In the pursuit of integrated schooling the Commission [for Racial Equality] has tried to ban some of our finest literature, change the names of our streets, turn Laburnum Grove into Botawangua Terrace. It has wanted to fill our schools with interpreters, teach lessons in foreign tongues, rewrite history. They have tried to turn Britain into a country where only aliens feel at home and the indigenous population become strangers in our own land. *(Daily Mail, 22 August 1990.)*

Education can be racist, as well as being a way to fight racism. The same attitudes can fester within classrooms as in the society outside.

> A schoolteacher who expects a black pupil to fail academically but to shine on the sporting field might not be greatly concerned when these expectations are met. The teacher's unthinking acceptance of the black pupil's academic failure removes some of the pressure for improvement — giving the black pupil 'permission' to fail. (Mary Warren, 'How to be Discriminating', New Internationalist, October 1983.)

● **Campaigning**

Another approach to combatting racism is to try to influence public opinion. But are we being naive in thinking that we can shift attitudes which have built up over four hundred years?

> At this time last year I touched on the growing concern for the environment; the 'Green' theme. During the intervening months, it has become a national unifying cause across political and community boundaries, and everyone has been made to feel that they can make some contribution. The challenge is shared, and is exciting. Creating the healthy environment of a multi-racial society can also be a unifying cause. (Michael Day, Chairman of the Commission for Racial Equality, CRE Annual Report 1989.)

A few years ago to be 'green' was to be a slightly mad hippy. Now it is so respectable that even Mrs Thatcher, a notoriously conservative ex-British prime minister, took up the environment as an important issue. Can racism be made into just as prominent an issue.

Striving for equality

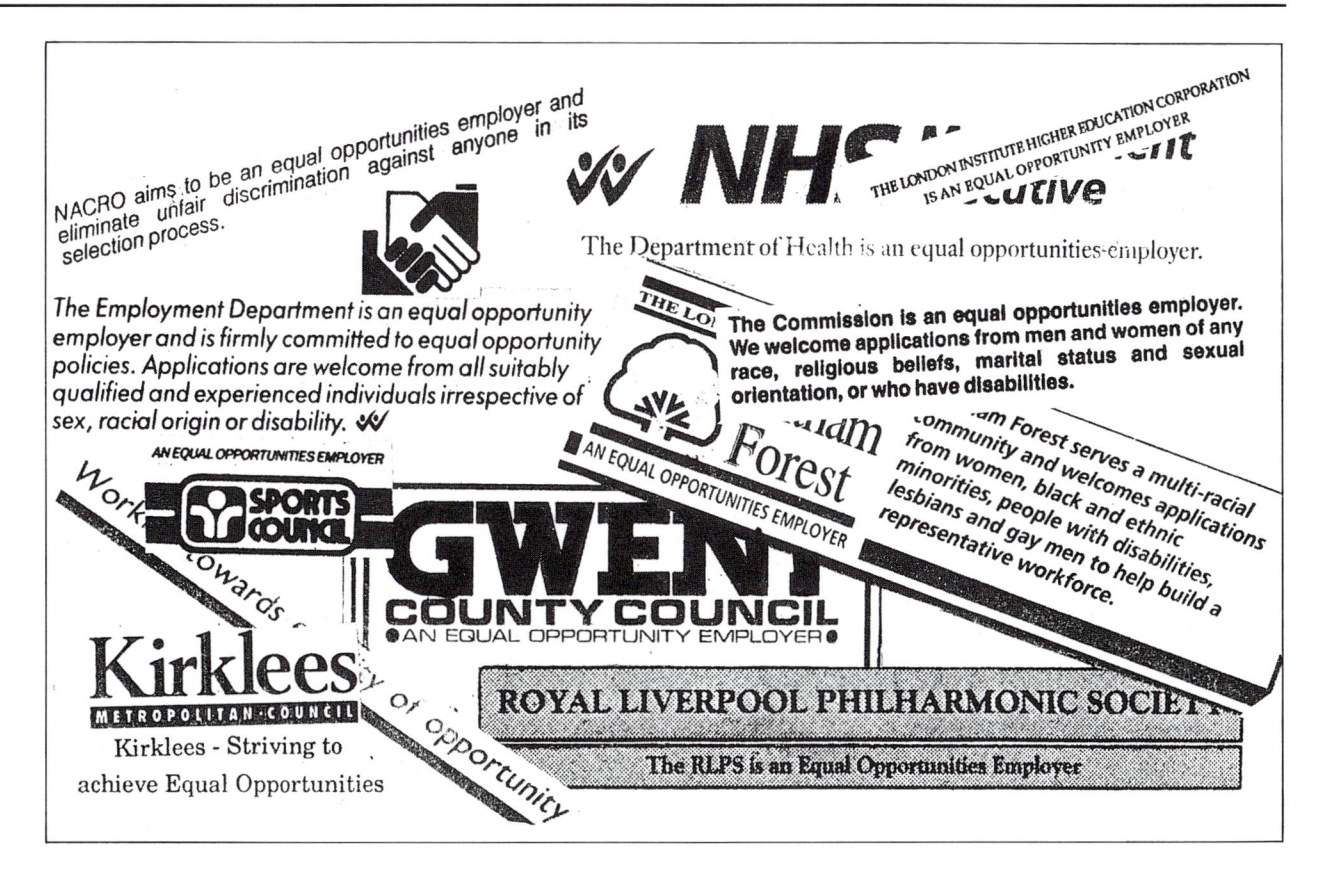

A collage of logos and statements from various organizations declaring themselves equal opportunities employers, including NACRO, NHS, The Department of Health, The Employment Department, The London Institute Higher Education Corporation, The Commission, Sports Council, Waltham Forest, Gwent County Council, Kirklees Metropolitan Council, and Royal Liverpool Philharmonic Society.

It has been proved that discrimination against black people in jobs continues to operate at a high level in spite of race relations laws. (See the information boxes on pages 7 and 8). People who have power to hire often favour those who are most like them. Organizations are trying to tackle this by having equal opportunity policies and by training managers so that they become aware of their hidden prejudices.

● **Equal opportunities policies**

Many companies and public organizations have started to introduce training programmes for their staff to ensure equal opportunities in employment, promotion and customer services. The effectiveness of these initiatives depends on white people giving up some of their power.

> Training whites to accept other races as equals under law in the United States [is] a gigantic undertaking shared in by thousands upon thousands of individuals, and hundreds of groups, organizations, and lawmakers ... It [is] certainly recognized that the essential element in race relations [is] behaviour, and behaviours [are] changed by law and public policy. Thus, training [that] combines knowledge of public policy and law with the technical skills and abilities of trainers to recognize, control and facilitate change on the basis of respect for individuals [is] critical. (John F. Coffey, 'Race Training in the United States: An Overview', *Strategies for Improving Race Relations: The Anglo-American Experience*, John W. Shaw et al.)

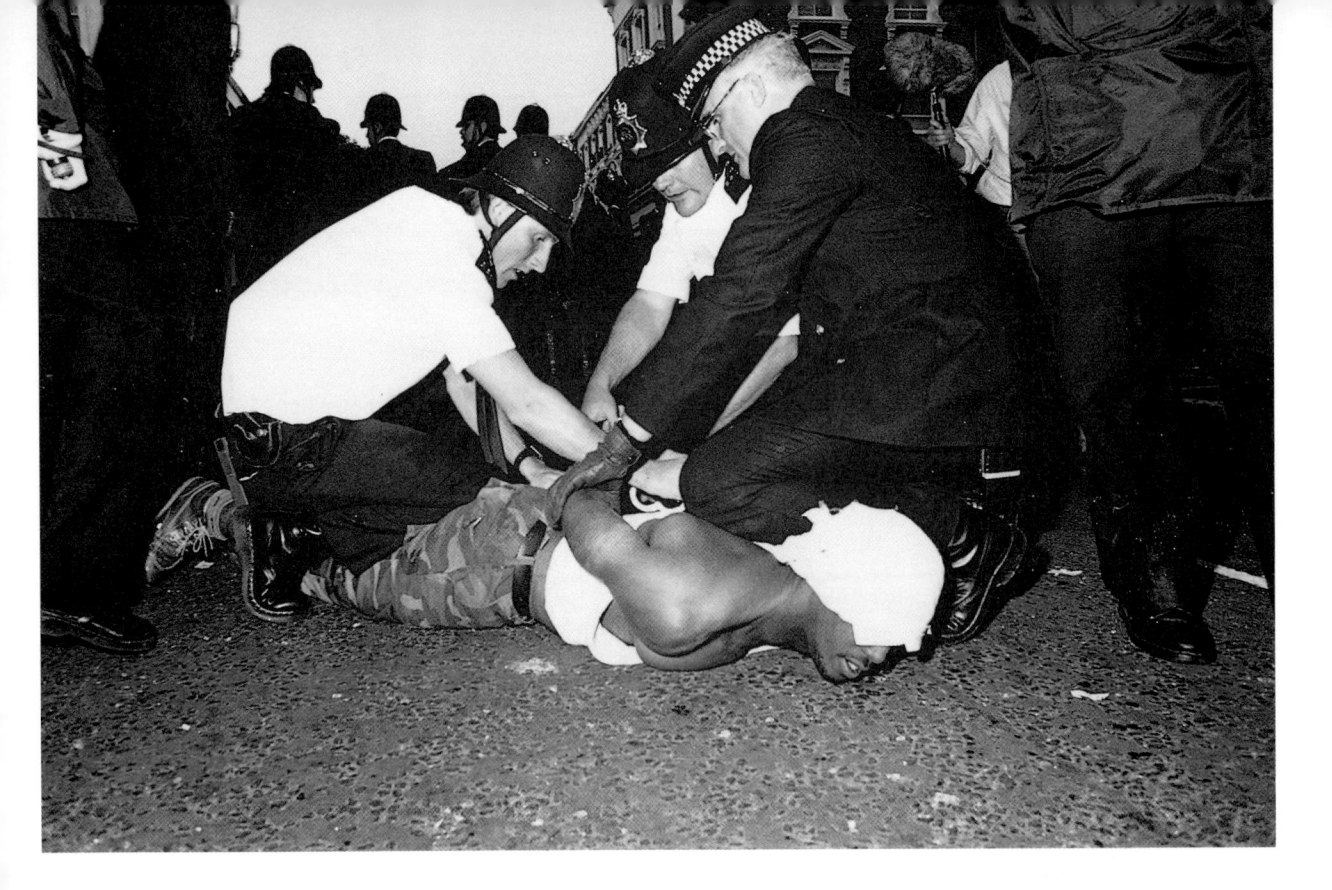

These measures have met with criticism from others:
> Such training is a mixture of pop psychology, race relations propaganda, and the systematic attempt to inculcate feelings of guilt in white people. It has been completely discredited by a very high proportion of those who have experienced it. (Ray Honeyford, letter to The Independent, 16 October 1990.)

● **Legislation**

Another approach favours using the law to fight discrimination and enforce equal rights.
> Law is among the most important means of ensuring equality between individuals and one of the most effective means of fighting racism ... It is not claimed that legislation can immediately eliminate prejudice. Nevertheless, by being a means of protecting the victims of acts based on prejudice, and by setting a moral example backed by the dignity of the courts, it can, in the long run, even change attitudes. *(UNESCO Statement on Race and Racial Prejudice, September 1967.)*

Others oppose using the law to combat discrimination because they say it interferes with the complex processes of free choice.

Above *Studies in Britain and the USA have shown that the people who operate the criminal justice system often act unfairly towards blacks. How can black people turn to the police and the courts for help if this is even partly true?*

Striving for equality

> Indeed, in questions of employment or accommodation it is extremely difficult to discern actual discrimination on racial grounds... Employers and landlords alike have to consider all sorts of criteria when they are making choices about people whom they employ or to whom they rent property. Most importantly, the freedom to choose is an essential prerequisite of a free society, and that ideal should remain paramount in our thinking on this matter. (K. Harvey Proctor and John R. Pinninger, *Immigration, Repatriation and the Commission for Racial Equality*, 1981.)

● Confrontation

Undoubtedly, the biggest challenge to racist behaviour has come from the disadvantaged communities themselves. In the 1960s the Civil Rights movement prompted change in the USA. The resistance of black South Africans led after decades to the crumbling of apartheid. In the early 1980s there were fiery street disturbances in many British towns.

Black resistance in South Africa to apartheid has been going on for decades. Ordinary people, often young children, took to the streets to protest against the racist system. Some were sent to prison, tortured or killed for these actions. It did not stop their fight for freedom and equality.

In the 1980s in Britain, angry black youths took to the streets, burning cars, attacking the police and destroying shops. It was their protest against years of oppression and discrimination.

> By the middle of the 1970s the youth had begun to emerge into the vanguard of the struggle. And they brought to it not only the traditions of their elders but an experience of their own . . . They were the 'burning spear' of the new resistance. The police took note, the state also . . . Among Asians too, it was the youth who were moving to the forefront of struggle. Like their Afro-Caribbean peers, they had been bred into a culture of racism and, like them, were impatient though not dismissive of the forms of struggle their elders conducted. (A. Sivanandan, *Resistance to Rebellion*, 1983.)

Not everyone agrees that we need to work harder to improve race relations:

> Black people should stop complaining about racism and get on with their lives. I want my people to stop crying. We don't need legislation to help us. Black people in Britain are as free as any other people. (Mr Glory Osaji-Umeaku, Founder of the Ethnic Harmony Campaign, quoted in *The Voice*, 4 September 1990.)

But Lord Scarman, a highly respected, white British judge who wrote a report on race riots that took place in Brixton, Britain in 1981, is in no doubt about the existence of racism. After revisiting Brixton in 1991, he wrote:

> Racial prejudice must be eliminated if racial disadvantage is to disappear. If we shirk this task, a very large number of valuable citizens will become embittered into being alienated from and hostile to the society of which they are members . . . (Lord Scarman, *Daily Telegraph*, 22 March 1991.)

---

1 *Have a debate in two groups about whether and how the anti-discrimination laws need to be changed in Britain.*

2 *Gandhi, whose political party played an important part in freeing India from British rule, said this about civilization. When asked what he thought of Western civilization, he replied that it would be a good idea. He also said that a civilization should be judged by its treatment of minorities. Do you think he is right? And if he is, is it fair to call any country that breeds racism civilized?*

7 Conclusions

Martin Luther King, a famous campaigner for human rights, said in a letter from a prison cell in Birmingham, Alabama, in 1963:

> We know through painful experience that freedom is never voluntarily given by the oppressor. It must be demanded by the oppressed. Frankly I have never yet engaged in a direct action movement that was 'well timed', according to the timetable of those who have not suffered unduly from the disease of segregation. For years now, I have heard the word 'Wait!' It rings in the ear of every Negro with a piercing familiarity. This 'Wait' has almost always meant 'Never' ... We must come to see with the distinguished jurist of yesterday that 'justice too long delayed is justice denied'. We have waited for more than 340 years for our constitutional and God given rights. *(The Essential Writings of Martin Luther King Jnr,* James M. Washington (ed.), 1986.)

A few months later, he made a speech that is now famous.

> So I say to you my friends that even though we must face the difficulties of today and tomorrow, I still have a dream. It is a dream deeply rooted in the American dream that one day this nation will rise up and live out the true meaning of its creed — we hold these truths to be self-evident, that all men are created equal ... I have a dream my four little children will one day live in a nation where they will not be judged by the colour of their skin but by the content of their character. I have a dream today! *(The Essential Writings of Martin Luther King Jnr.)*

Martin Luther King, second from the left on the front row, leading the 'March on Washington' in 1963 to demand equal rights for black people.

Nelson Mandela, a champion of the anti-apartheid movement, was released after spending twenty-five years in prison for fighting against apartheid. In 1991, as president of the African National Congress, he began negotiating the future of South Africa with the white political party who put him in prison.

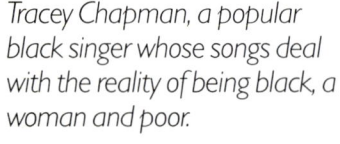

Tracey Chapman, a popular black singer whose songs deal with the reality of being black, a woman and poor.

The split between black and white is what Nelson Mandela has spent his life fighting against.

> During my lifetime I dedicated my life to the struggle of the African people. I have fought against white domination. I have cherished the ideal of a democratic and free society in which all persons live together in harmony with equal opportunities. It is an ideal which I hope to live for, and to see realized. But my lord, if needs be, it is an ideal for which I am prepared to die. (Nelson Mandela, speaking to a South African court at his trial for treason in 1964.)

These powerful statements are as valid today throughout the world as they were then. The history and politics of both Europe and America are stained with the blood of slavery, and black people are still subject to racism throughout their lives. In the words of a well-known song:

> Across the lines
> Who would dare to go
> Under the bridge
> Over the tracks
> That separate whites from blacks?
>
> Choose sides
> Or run for your life
> Tonight the riots begin
> On the back streets of America
> They kill the dream of America.

(Tracy Chapman, *Across the Lines*, 1988.)

Conclusions

In a world where the old certainties of East-West conflict have ended, there is a danger that new global hatred could emerge along racial or ethnic lines. In Europe there is talk of a white 'fortress Europe' already, in spite of the fact that 16 million Europeans are not white. A firm and explicit rejection of racism will prevent such hatreds taking new root. James Baldwin uses an image from the Bible, of a second purging of the earth similar to the one that caused Noah and his sons to build the ark, to warn of the need to fight racism:

> Everything now, we must assume, is in our hands; we have no right to assume otherwise. If we — and now I mean the relatively conscious whites and the relatively conscious blacks, who must, like lovers, insist on, or create, the consciousness of the others — do not falter in our duty now, we may be able ... to end the racial nightmare ... and change the history of the world. If we do not now dare everything, the fulfilment of that prophecy, re-created from the Bible in a song by a slave, is upon us: God gave Noah the rainbow sign, No more water, the fire next time!
> (James Baldwin, *The Fire Next Time*, 1964.)

Political change in South Africa makes little difference unless economic power is also more equally shared. Until that happens, political and legal declarations will be just empty words, as they are for most black people. They will just be looking through the fence at what they are denied.

Glossary

Afro-Caribbeans People with family origins in the Caribbean, descended from Africans.
Alien A person regarded by others as an outsider, not belonging to their society or country.
Apartheid A political system developed in South Africa that legally separates racial groups and gives each group different rights. White people have all the advantages.
Asians People with family origins in the Indian sub-continent.
Black people A term which refers to all non-white people.
Caste system A Hindu practice based on the belief that people divide into different levels of humanity, which are determined by birth.
Citizen A member of a society, or resident in a country, whose rights and obligations are defined by law.
Civil Rights movement The campaign in the USA which in the 1960s fought for and won equal legal rights for black people.
Colonialism The economic and political domination of one country by another, and all the ideas that support this.
Culture The traditions, values, beliefs and lifestyles shared by a group of people.
Empire A group of separate territories controlled by a dominant country.
Equality of opportunity The social and legal conditions under which every person has an equal chance to succeed and progress, without barriers of prejudice.
Ethnic minority A racial or cultural group living in a society where the majority of the population has different cultural roots.
European Community The federation of some major European states with shared economic and political objectives.
Genocide An attempt to destroy a racial, ethnic, religious or national group.
Guest worker A foreign worker employed in a country but given few citizenship rights and expected to return later to his or her own country.
Ideology A body of ideas based on the beliefs of a powerful group.
Immigrants People who for political, religious or economic reasons move from their country of birth to another.
Indigenous population People living in a country where their ancestors originated.
Integration The mixing of different racial, ethnic and religious groups in everyday life.
Nazism A racial ideology and political system based on the theory that certain types of white people are superior to all other people and particularly to Jews, and have the right to exterminate them.
Parochialism Lack of concern with events outside your own immediate experience.
Pernicious Evil.
Prejudice Making a judgement about something, using inadequate information or false ideas.
Race A term commonly used to describe a group of people who share some inherited characteristics. Years ago, races were seen as fundamental biological divisions of humankind, but scientific evidence has disproved this.
Racial disadvantage The experience of people who are treated unequally and unfairly because of their racial background.
Racial discrimination Unfair treatment of people because of their racial origins.
Racial harmony An absence of conflict between racial and ethnic groups.
Racism The belief that one race is superior to another.
Refugee A person who flees from his or her country because of fear of prosecution or as a result of a disaster.
Scapegoat A person who is made to take the blame for problems which are not their fault.
Segregation The enforced separation of different racial, ethnic or religious groups.
White people A term used to refer to all people with family origins in Europe.
Xenophobia A hatred of foreigners.

Further reading

Baldwin, James *The Fire Next Time* (Penguin, 1964)
Benedict, Ruth *Race and Racism* (Routledge & Kegan Paul, 1983)
Fryer, Peter *Staying Power: The History of Black People in Britain* (Pluto, 1984)
Gordon, Paul and Newnham, Anne *Different Worlds: Racism and Discrimination in Britain* (Runnymede Trust, 1986)
Green, Jonathan *Them: Voices from the Immigrant Community in Contemporary Britain* (Secker & Warburg, 1990)
Institute of Race Relations *Roots of Racism; Patterns of Racism; How Racism Came to Britain; The Fight Against Racism,* a series of four books (1982)
Vadgama, Kusoom *India in Britain* (Robert Royce, 1984)
Williams, Juan *Eyes on the Prize: America's Civil Rights Years 1954-1965* (Harrap, 1988)
Wright, Richard *Black Boy* (Penguin, 1970)

Picture acknowledgements

All artwork by Steve Wheele. The publishers gratefully acknowledge permission from the following to reproduce their photos in this book: Benetton 35; Chapel Studios 12, 44 (top); Eye Ubiquitous 13, 29; Hulton-Deutsch Collection 22 (bottom), 25 (top); Impact 5, 15, 36, 42; Living Marxism (Simon Norfolk) *cover,* 4 (both), 21, 25, 28, 30; Billie Love 14, 17; Photri 18, 19, 23, 34, 43; Popperfoto 11, 37; Rex Features 20, 24, 33 (both), 41, 44; Topham Picture Library 8, 10, 26, 31, 32, 38; Wayland Picture Library 6, 16, 22 (top), 45.

Contact addresses

Each of these organizations can provide figures on the effects of racism, as well as articles and books about it:

Australia
Office of Multicultural Affairs, 3-5 National Court, Canberra ACT 2600.

Canada
Urban Alliance of Race Relations, Suite 203, 675 King St West, Toronto, Ontario M5V 1M9.

UK
Runnymede Trust, 11 Princelet St, London E1 6QH.

USA
National Association for the Advancement of Colored Peoples, 260 Fifth Avenue, New York NY 10001.

Index

Numbers in **bold** refer to pictures as well as text.

American racism 5, 15, 27
Amin, Idi see *Uganda*
Australian aborigines 9

Benetton advertising **35**
Birmingham, Alabama, USA 15
British racists, (interviewed) 4
Bronx, The **5**, **15**

Canadian racism 15, 27
caste system **13**, 14
civilization, origins of 18, 19
Civil Rights movement **10**, **37**, 41, **43**
colonialism 6, **14**

demonstrations
  anti racism **4**, **30**, **33**
  racist ***cover picture***, **4**, **28**

education 36-8
  and the American Civil Rights campaign **37**
equality of opportunity in employment 7, 8, 12, **39**, 40, 41
European post-Second World War reconstruction 8

Geldof, Bob and racism **20**, 21

Handsworth, Britain **42**
health care 15
Hispanic population in USA **15**
Hong Kong **23**, 24
housing **5**, **25**, 41

immigrants 21, **22**, 23, **32**
  Arab immigrants to France **8**
  European perceptions of 23, 24
  from Hong Kong to Britain **23**, 24
  Turkish immigrants to Germany **32**, **33**

Jung, Carl 18

King, Martin Luther **43**

Lee, Spike **26**
legal system and racism **11**, 29, 30, 34, 40
le Pen, Jean Marie 8, **24**

Mandela, Nelson **44**
Maori experience of racism 27, 30
media racism 21, 22, 26
Morris, Bill **31**

Native Americans 5, **18**, 27

origins of racism 7, **9**, 17

Powell, Enoch 22
power and racism **11**
Pyramids, The **19**

racism
  among academics 17
  characteristics of **5**, **9**, 10, 15, 19, 27
  definition of 10
racist humour 8, 25, 26

Saddique, Nasreen 28
Sekhon, Kuldip Singh, murder of 25
slave auction **6**
slavery **6**, 7
South Africa **16**, **17**, 27, 44, **45**

Thatcher, Margaret 20, **21**
Thomas, Judge Clarence **34**

Uganda, expulsion of Asians **12**
Ullah, Ahmed, killing of 29
untouchables see *caste system*

Winfrey, Oprah **33**